W9-ADO-442

The GREAT AMERICAN PICKUP TRUCK

Stylesetter, Workhorse, Sport Truck

Henry Rasmussen

Motorbooks International
Publishers & Wholesalers Inc
Osceola, Wisconsin 54020, USA ®

First published in 1988 by Motorbooks International Publishers & Wholesalers Inc, P O Box 2, 729 Prospect Avenue, Osceola, WI 54020 USA
© Henry Rasmussen, 1988
Reprinted fall 1991
Motorbooks International is a certified trademark, registered with the United States Patent Office
Printed and bound in Hong Kong
The information in this book is true and complete to the best of our knowledge. All recommendations are made without any guarantee on the part of the author or publisher, who also disclaim any liability incurred in connection with the use of this data or specific details
We recognize that some words, model names and designations, for example, mentioned herein are the property of various automotive and component manufacturers. We use them for identification purposes only. This is not an official publication
Library of Congress Cataloging-in-Publication Data
Rasmussen, Henry.
  The great American pickup truck : stylesetter, workhorse, sport
truck / photography by Henry Rasmussen.
    p.   cm.
  ISBN 0-87938-307-0
  1. Trucks—United States—History.   I. Title.
TL230.R38 1988
629.2'23—dc19   88-11733
                                         CIP
Motorbooks International books are also available at discounts in bulk quantity for industrial or sales-promotional use. For details write to Special Sales Manager at the Publisher's address

On the cover, a bird's-eye view of Florida collector Sonny Glasbrenner's rare 1938 Mack Jr. *On the back cover,* Kevin Martin and his 1981 Toyota 4x4 play in the sand at California's Pismo Beach. *On the frontis-piece,* a 1941 Plymouth shows off its polished Sunday suit. *On the title page,* the colorful profiles of three of the most collectible Chevys from the fifties. *On this page,* man's best friends are his dog and his pickup—Bud Bixler tours the back country with Jake and his 1959 Chevy four-wheel-drive. *On the following spread,* Cliff Palmer and his co-driver—both residents of Chama, New Mexico—pose with their well-worn 1930 Model A Ford. *On the last page,* the face of a 1948 Studebaker, with its fashionably faired-in headlights.

Contents

1

From primitive workhorse to extravagant playmate

At the turn of the century, once the horseless carriage had become firmly established, it did not take long before entrepreneurial minds began to realize the new invention's potential for hauling goods.

Such early endeavors brought forth the 1903 Bosworth, powered by steam and featuring a diminutive delivery box at the rear. The contraption did not progress beyond the prototype stage, however, but others did. Among these pioneers was Cadillac, which began manufacturing a line of light trucks in 1904.

Of the manufacturers still involved in building commercial vehicles, Ford was the first to offer such a product. Introduced in 1905, it was called the Commercial Car, and only ten were built that year. Dodge began producing light trucks in 1917. The next year, Chevrolet jumped on the bandwagon.

The most pickup-like of these vehicles were, to begin with, listed in the catalogs under the type designation express. The distinction of having first used the actual pickup designation may belong to International. This company, referring to its initial effort as Auto Wagon, entered the field in 1907.

In 1921, International introduced a smaller and faster type of light truck, designated the Model S. The S stood for Speedtruck, and the machine chugged along at an impressive pace of 25 mph. One of the body configurations listed was called pickup; thus was born a term that in due time would come to describe one of the most useful types of vehicles.

The pickup, to begin with, was certainly meant for utility use only. As such, it was—and continued to be, long into the postwar period—a primitive machine. The steering was heavy, the suspension hard and the comfort features nonexistent. The pickup was indeed a mechanized workhorse.

But a curious thing happened. The person who used the pickup to do a job grew fond of the hardy machine, and soon found it useful beyond the farm and the construction site. On weekends, it was perfect for taking the family picnicking.

Subsequently, a new generation discovered new playgrounds for aging pickups. Digging them out of the junkyards, these young enthusiasts put the derelicts back on active duty, where they began serving the needs of a new lifestyle.

The pickup became a cult object. It was seen on the beaches, loaded with surfboards and sun-loving companions. It roamed the forests and riverbeds, where its owner flogged it heartlessly—just for the fun of it. And it appeared in the custom car shows.

Observing these trends, manufacturers could hardly afford to sit idle. Responding to what they saw as a new market, they soon brought forth designs to fit the changing bill. The oil crisis caused further refinement of the product, spawning the development of smaller pickups.

Today, the machine comes in all sizes, shapes and colors, eminently suited for all purposes—work and play, and all the shades in between. It is either full-size or compact, has two- or four-wheel-drive capacity, is endowed with awesome trailering ability or breathtaking performance, and comes with interiors that range from no-frills to ultra-plush.

It's no wonder that the light truck has become a best seller. In the United States, sales for 1986 totaled 4.6 million units, or nearly one third of the automotive market.

It is hoped the enthusiast with an eye for nostalgia and a mind for the novel will enjoy this portrait of the pickup—America's beloved workhorse and playmate.

2

A grand-daddy who's still roaming dusty backroads

Henry Ford—not the inventor of the automobile as much as the instigator of its mass production—fittingly was also a pioneer of the commercial vehicle. After a false start in 1905, he reintroduced his Commercial Car in 1912. It was now based on the Model T, which had been introduced in 1908, and was the machine that changed the habits of a nation and a world.

The man on the street used his ingenious ways to fashion Ford's car to fit his own particular needs. And so it was actually his customers, as much as his competition, who forced Ford to build a pickup-type vehicle.

The first true Ford pickup arrived in 1925, and consisted of an optional box mounted on the Runabout chassis. As many as 34,000 units were made that first year; the next two years saw total production soar to more than 100,000. The pickup cost $281 in 1925. Today, a restored example will set the buyer back at least thirty times that amount.

The pickup grand-daddy pictured on this and the following spread belongs to Ralph "Whitey" Wescott, owner of a salvage yard in Largo, Florida. The 1926 Model T was at one point during its long life fitted with a conversion pickup box, complete with protective lid. Now restored according to Wescott's wishes—specifically for the purpose of being used on the road, and not for show—the rugged survivor is driven daily by its jovial owner.

Drivers of the sophisticated pickups of the eighties would feel thoroughly out of place behind the wheel of the distant forefather of the breed, the Ford Model T of the twenties, pictured on the preceding pages. Mounted on the column are such oddities as a manual thottle lever and a spark regulator. On the floor, above, the operator encounters a cluster of three pedals. Depressing the one on the left places the contraption in low gear. Letting it up engages high gear—fortunately there are only two forward gears to choose from. Reverse is reached by depressing the pedal in the middle. Unfortunately, the brake pedal is located all the way to the right, exactly where the gas pedal is found on a modern car. Most confusing. Well, with just 22 hp and 1600 rpm at the driver's disposal—and a top speed of 26 mph—the damage resulting from a misplaced foot is relatively minor. Pictured to the left, owner Whitey Wescott prepares to turn.

3

Fading fast but not forgotten

The back roads of America constitute the greatest of museums—a veritable paradise for the automotive archaeologist. A trip through the countryside becomes a trip through history. Along the dusty roadsides, inside thickets of young trees, behind dilapidated barns, all kinds of curious objects lie hidden—rusty relics of an industrial revolution.

Together with tractors and other farm implements, the pickup is the favorite object of the backyard collector. And no wonder. This versatile vehicle, an amalgamation of tool and toy, plays a part in the nostalgic remembrances of almost every child.

Memories of the sunny, carefree days of the past are, in the mind of the enthusiast, combined with an appreciation for things mechanical. There's a dream of recapturing this romance of a bygone era through the resurrection of an inanimate object. A simplistic explanation, perhaps. But why is the countryside decorated with these rusty old relics? Just because they sit untouched year after year does not mean the dreams are dead.

A pickup derelict, no matter the degree of emaciation, is always alive. It is guarded jealously, sometimes to the tune of a shotgun. And the plans for its rejuvenation, should the traveler happen to strike up a conversation with the owner, are precise and plentiful. Thus, although the condition can be deceptively faded, a seemingly abandoned pickup is certainly never forgotten.

*F*ound abandoned in a field near Salinas, California, the 1936 Ford V-8 pickup featured on the chapter opening spread is as charming a derelict as one is ever likely to run across—rust, cracked windshield and all. It was the only year for this particular style of grille. Note the single wiper; the second wiper was an option. Captured on the previous spread, a 1947 Hudson Coupe Express pickup. It was the last year for the Hudson's commercial line, and just 2,917 units were made. Capacity was three-quarter-ton, wheelbase, 128 inches. The 212 ci straight six—with a block of chrome alloy—produced 102 hp at 4000 rpm. The fading survivor, found in Largo, Florida, is no match for the climate of the region, with its rust-promoting humidity and voracious foliage. Pictured to the left, another example of the coincidental beauty of corrosion. The victim is an early-postwar Dodge. Above, a Ford from the late forties or early fifties has had its engine replaced by weeds—talk about flower power!

4

A relentless pursuer of the classic pickup

Like its passenger car cousin, the pickup reached its classic high point with the period beginning in the late twenties and lasting to the early forties—the end coinciding with the outbreak of World War II and the general changeover to production of war materiel.

During the early part of this period, the pickup remained a reworked passenger car, using its chassis, grille, hood, fenders and cab. Gradually, however, the light truck took on a shape of its own, although a relationship with the passenger lines of the respective manufacturers remained close.

By the mid-thirties, the light truck had generally become a separate entity, a cross between a passenger car and a larger truck.

The classic era was populated by many great names. Unfortunately, most of these eventually faded from the scene. Diamond T stood out as one of the most herculean of the breed. Studebaker, Hudson, Willys, Federal, REO—all had their heydays during this heady era. One of the most select pickups a person could own in the late twenties was a Buddy Stewart, built by the Stewart Motor Corporation in Buffalo, New York.

Sonny Glasbrenner does not own a Buddy Stewart—yet. But the classic pickups he and his wife, Merrilu, display in their sprawling garage in Seminole, Florida—a collection gathered through the dogged persistence of true enthusiasm—are worthy of the close look presented on the following pages.

Glasbrenner found his half-ton 1935 Series C-1 International, shown on the chapter opening spread, in Virginia, where he bought it from the second owner. The original paint and the pristine wood in the cab superstructure were telltale signs of a meticulously maintained vehicle. Having received a complete restoration, the survivor has now attained the coveted status of an AACA (Antique Automobile Club of America) Senior. Dodge introduced an attractive new line of light trucks in 1933. With their sloping radiator grilles, these machines looked similar to the Dodge passenger cars. But by 1935, the year of the pickup featured on the previous spread, the styling of the passenger cars had been updated, causing the commercial line to lag behind. Nevertheless, the old design made for a handsome truck, with Dodge's ram leaping aggressively from the radiator cap, as seen in the photograph on this page. The half-ton KC series pickup is powered by an inline six, displacing 201 ci and producing 70 hp at 3500 rpm.

GMC joined the ranks of commercial
vehicle manufacturers as late as 1920. The
firm revamped the styling of its light trucks
in 1936, fitting round fenders and a fancy
grille, which featured an intricate design of
horizontal and vertical bars, as seen in the
photograph above. Glasbrenner bought this
rare long-wheelbase example in Alabama,
where it at one point had served in the
state's public road works. The bright yellow
it had donned for this purpose had been
added directly on top of factory-fresh black

paint, he discovered during the course of the
resurrection process. Today, the perfectly
restored survivor, a recent AACA national
winner, is as good as new—or better. Under
the hood rests a flathead Olds powerplant—
GMC did not build a power source of its
own at the time. Displacement of the
straight six is 230 ci and output 86 hp at
3600 rpm. Notice that Glasbrenner
emphasized the heavy-duty character of the
machine by fitting mud-type tires at the
rear.

*M*ack is a legendary name among builders of heavy trucks. That the company also marketed a small half-ton truck is little known. Prospering throughout the twenties, Mack, like so many others—among them REO—fell on hard times during the thirties. Giving REO something to build, and Mack something to sell, the companies joined in a venture that produced a line of light trucks. Thus, by 1935, a disguised REO was introduced as the Mack Jr. In 1937, a revised model made its debut. New hood

and grille were among the exterior changes. Glasbrenner's 1938 example, pictured on this and the previous spread, sports an inline six-cylinder Continental under the hood. Displacement is 206 ci and output 72 hp at 3000 rpm. The Mack Bulldog is proudly carried atop the radiator, left, and the Mack Jr. insignias are prominently displayed on the grille, the hood sides and the wheel covers—as well as on the gauges, as seen in the photograph above.

*F*ord's venerable Model T pickup lasted until 1927. When the Model A pickup arrived the following year, the machine was still not entirely new, stubbornly featuring what was essentially the old Model T Runabout body mounted on a redesigned chassis. But progress could not be halted for long—while the early Fords could only be had in black, by the end of the Model A life span, in 1931, Ford pickups were offered in thirty-eight colors, varying from Yukon Yellow to Rubelite Red. In 1932, it was time for the next step—the introduction of the V-8 engine. The grille finally became slanted, as dictated by the changing flow of fashion. By 1937, Ford passenger cars had received further streamlining, featuring a sharply pointed grille. But, as far as the commercial line was concerned, the new design was only applied to the delivery trucks; the pickups sported a grille shared with Ford's line of heavier trucks. As seen in the photograph on this spread, the design was a bit awkward, and gave this pickup, a 1939 vintage, a rather nose-heavy appearance.

30

*B*etween the years of 1935 and 1941, Chrysler marketed light trucks under the Plymouth badge. To begin with, these vehicles were based on the passenger model, but from 1937 on, a new type was introduced, built on its own platform. In 1939, a second line based on the smallest Dodge truck chassis was added. The latter was styled like the passenger cars, while the line built on the lighter chassis kept the styling of the commercial line, with the headlights mounted between the fenders and the hood. Among slight styling revisions for 1941, the headlights were moved to the crest of the fenders, giving this model year a wide-eyed appearance. Power came from a straight six, displacing 201 ci and producing 87 hp at 3800 rpm. Glasbrenner's rare machine is a 1941 model, the last year, of which just 6,269 units—a panel delivery version included— were built.

32

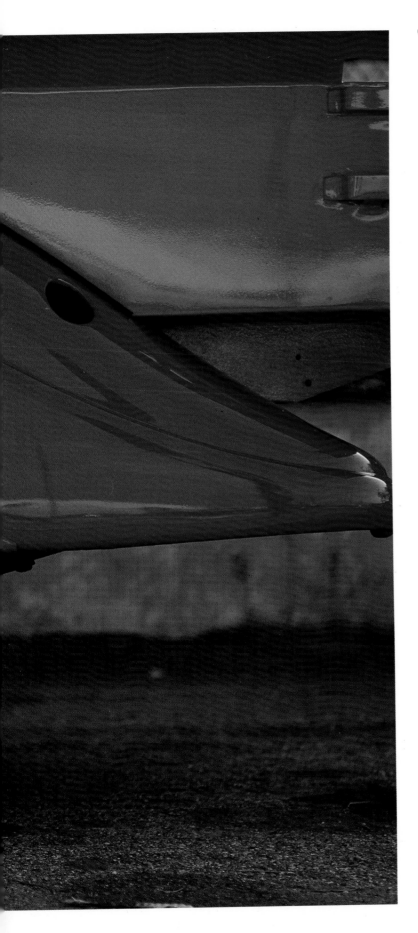

5

Terraplane—bizarre, but eternally beautiful

Incorporated in 1909, the Hudson Motor Car Company in 1919 introduced a new line of cars, the Essex, which immediately proved itself to be a resounding success. The first light trucks, arriving in 1929, were based on the Essex chassis but marketed under a separate name, the Dover.

The bold experimentation with badge identity was continued when, in the early thirties—production had dwindled to 412 units in 1931, and zero in 1932—the Terraplane name was added to the Essex badge. Then, for 1934, the Essex was dropped altogether, and the scene was set for what many consider the most beautiful pickup of all time.

The man responsible for the dazzling looks of the Terraplane was Frank Spring. An engineer as well as stylist—he was thoroughly familiar with all aspects of aircraft and automobile design—Spring had joined Hudson as its chief stylist in 1931.

A forerunner in the field of aerodynamics, Spring gave his creations smooth, sweeping lines of a grace and boldness seen only on the most advanced European sports cars of the day. Thus, the pickup, directly based on the Terraplane passenger car, also became extremely advanced.

At the time, to many, this futuristic look seemed too daring—simply a bit bizarre. But, as is often the case, posterity tends to produce a more mature perspective. Today, the Terraplane pickup has proven itself to be a design that will surely stand up to the test of time.

*O*nly three examples of the 1934 Terraplane pickup are known to exist: one in Utah, one in Arizona, one in southern California. The latter is featured on these pages, where it is photographed as it stands, undergoing a frame-up restoration. Seen on the previous spread, a close-up of the sweeping rear fender, with its optional wheel cover. On this spread, a three-quarter frontal view, revealing the smooth shape of the grille, with its fan-shaped arrangement of vertical bars—painted black on the commercial line, chromed on the passenger line. The headlights are still to be mounted. In 1935, a new grille was tried, but the Terraplane—a fabulous name indeed— lasted just one more year. On the following spread, a three-quarter rear view. The pointed tails of the rear fenders are supposed to be connected by a streamlined piece of sheet metal—an item still to be attached. Owner Press Kale views the exquisite design from his vantage point in the doorway.

6

Crosley: a matter of too little, too early

By the mid-thirties, Powell Crosley had made his fortune manufacturing radios and refrigerators. Today, these products are forgotten, but his name lives on, thanks to his two obsessions—baseball and cars. Crosley was the owner of the Cincinnati Redlegs; Crosley Field is named after him. And there are his curious little cars, all bearing a Crosley badge, still to be seen wherever car enthusiasts gather.

The dream of manufacturing his own car became a reality in 1939. It was a two-cylinder air-cooled machine, billed as the economy car of the future. Inevitably, the war put a halt to the project.

But Crosley was back in 1946. To begin with, a car-hungry public snapped up the curious little creations. The engine was now a water-cooled four-cylinder unit, the revolutionary design featuring a sheet-metal block. The block turned out to be an easy victim of corrosion, however, and word about its reliability problem spread quickly.

Added to this was the public's fascination with the V-8, and the impressive automobiles it powered— luxurious "spaceships"—which soon flooded the market. Nothing could stop the ultimate disaster. By 1952, after having produced 70,000 units, the company went belly up.

As a pickup, Crosley's little machine precluded the ultimate rise of the mini truck by some thirty years. Unfortunately, his dream was a matter of too little, too early.

In the picture above, the narrow little
Crosley cuts a comical figure. Although
passenger cars were built already in 1946,
commercial vehicles did not become
available until 1947—the unit featured here
represents that first year of production.
Owner Tom DeJohn of Menlo Park,
California, peers through the diminutive rear
window. He found the Crosley parked on a
street in San Francisco, where kids had
been allowed to turn the little machine on
its side. The owner obviously did not care
for it anymore, so DeJohn coughed up $450
and proceeded to give the survivor a
complete restoration. The result was a Best
of Show at the 1987 meet of the West
Coast Chapter of the Crosley Automobile
Club. Beyond the firewall rests a fierce little
engine, displacing 44 ci and producing 26
hp at 5600 rpm, shown to the left. On the
following spread, a close-up of the Crosley's
dash, with its sparse but complete
instrumentation. On the floor, a stick
connects with a three-speed
nonsynchromesh box.

7

Old faces make a comeback before new ones set off a boom

The war was over. A promise of peace and prosperity permeated the air, and the soldiers came home from the front, returning to the farms and factories. It was time to get the country back on the road. It was time to get the wheels rolling again.

With the public bursting from a pent-up demand for cars, caused by the halt in civilian production during the war, the advent of peace brought on feverish activity in Detroit.

But the first pickups to venture out that early spring were not fresh new faces. While engineers and stylists were sent back to the drawing boards to produce new designs, the tools and the dies that had been used to build the prewar models were dusted off.

Chevrolet came out with a line that had first been seen in 1941. Dodge stayed with the look it had developed for 1939. And International reintroduced its 1940 models. The only face to look fairly new was that of Ford, which brought out a design conceived as late as 1942.

It would take three years before entirely new lines of pickups began to show up on the postwar roads. That's when the market exploded. Chevrolet, for instance, went from an annual production of 171,000 units in 1946, to 414,000 in 1950. Thus, the immediate postwar era was a good one, a period producing memorable machinery—and paving the way for the great fifties.

*W*ith its characteristic waterfall grille, its close-set, faired-in headlights and its decorative, two-tone paint scheme, Ford gave its pickup a look that resulted in a high recognition factor. Restored to perfection by a Florida collector, the 1946 example featured on the previous spread was painted in its original colors—Glade Green with Tacoma Cream accents. When the model was replaced in 1948, about 75,000 units had been built of the half-ton pickup. The customer had a choice of two engines: an L-head six, displacing 226 ci and producing 95 hp at 3300 rpm, or a 239 ci L-head V-8, which managed 100 hp at 3800 rpm. Seen on this spread, the contrast between perfectly restored and perfectly rough. To the left, the immaculate whitewall beauty of the 1946 Ford described above. To the right, the weathered, four-decade patina of a 1946 International.

The photographs on this spread feature views of a 1946 International. With its bulbous fenders and faired-in headlights, it reflected passenger car styling of the late thirties. Introduced in 1940, the model stayed in production until 1949. The half-ton pickup cost $640 in 1941. In 1946, the numbers on the price tag had changed to $930. Putting as many as 113,000 units on the road in 1946—counting all types of light trucks—International was off to a good start, placing fourth after Chevrolet, Ford and Dodge. The example featured here, photographed in California's Napa Valley, has certainly taken a beating over the years. But the International badge—in the photograph to the left—with its row of three diamonds, is surprisingly well preserved. The pickup was powered by a straight six— promoted under the trade name Green Diamond—with a displacement of 213 ci and an output of 82 hp at 3200 rpm.

*D*iamond T trucks have a long and distinguished history, dating back as far as 1911. Built in Chicago, the machine soon became famous for its high-quality and rugged construction. Referred to as the Rolls-Royce of trucks, the Diamond T featured comfortable interiors and beautiful styling. While the emphasis was on larger-type trucks, the company for a number of years built pickups on a chassis as small as three-quarter-ton. When reintroduced after the war, the styling appeared somewhat dated, but the quality and the prestige were still there. The series 201 survivor seen on this spread is a one-ton unit from 1948, and unrestored—with the exception of a paint job. It came originally from the oilfields of Oklahoma. Under that long, pointed hood rests a six-cylinder Continental. The series was discontinued in 1951, after which date no light trucks were made. In 1967, the company merged with REO, and re-emerged as Diamond Reo.

Studebaker goes all the way back to 1852, when Henry and Clem Studebaker opened a blacksmith shop in South Bend, Indiana. The company specialized in horse-drawn wagons, and ultimately became the largest manufacturer of such vehicles in the world. The first horseless carriage emerged in 1902. Over the next three decades, Studebaker's chassis proved to be a popular foundation for commercial vehicles, but it was in 1937 that the company first began offering a pickup—the beautiful Coupe Express. The K-10 pickup was introduced in 1938, but was replaced in 1941 by the Model M5. Re-emerging in 1946, the M5 was built in a moderate volume of 14,000 units that year. The example seen here, found in North Carolina, is a 1948 model, a year in which production fell to just over 10,000 units. Below the new paint, the beautiful truck is all original, with just 15,000 miles on the odometer. Power comes from a 169 ci L-head six, producing 80 hp at 4000 rpm. New pickup models were introduced in 1949, 1954 and 1960, until the end came in 1964.

*P*ictured on this spread, the second-generation postwar Ford—the first designed after the war—the Model F-1, introduced in 1948. The styling was bold, and expressed power and heavy-duty sentiments in an exceptionally successful way. The model received a new grille in 1951, a design lasting until 1953, when Ford delivered the ultimate knockout blow in the form of the F-100. The example seen here is from 1949; total production of the F-1, in all its various configurations, amounted to 105,000 units that year. The pickup cost $1,302. Power, as with the model it replaced, came in two shapes. The bottom choice was Ford's 226 ci L-head six, producing 95 hp at 3300 rpm. The top selection consisted of the company's popular 239 ci V-8, generating an even 100 hp at 3800 rpm. The powertrain also came in two options—three-speed automatic or four-speed manual. The convenience options included such amenities as illuminated cigar lighter and leather-covered armrests.

Overshadowing its Ford competitor, Chevrolet's Advance-Design light truck—bowing in the summer of 1947—has become the pickup of the era with the most lasting impact on the American landscape. Still today, with nearly two million units placed on the road during the six-year life of the model, one cannot travel the highways and byways of the United States without encountering a steady—albeit thinning—flow of these faithful survivors. The styling was exceptionally clean, with a natural rhythm to the lines, although not as bold as the ones found on the Ford. The example featured here is a 3100 series half-ton pickup from 1953, the last year. Power came from the 235 ci Thriftmaster six, producing 112 hp at 3700 rpm. Heavy-duty three- or four-speed transmissions were available, with the gearshift lever located on the column. Chrome grille was optional, as were chrome bumpers and chrome hubcaps. Optional whitewall tires were available for that final touch of class.

58

*D*odge came out of the war a winner. The
company had built 400,000 military
trucks—a fleet of vehicles that had proved
their mettle in a confidence-boosting
manner. Thanks to a well-planned
changeover to civilian operation and the
prestige earned on the battlefield, Dodge
moved into third position among US
manufacturers, with a 1946 output of nearly
150,000 units. The company introduced its
first postwar design in 1948. As was the
fashion, the new style featured pontoon
fenders with faired-in headlights. Three
vertical bars accentuated the grille. This
element was redesigned for 1951—an
example of that year's B-3-B half-ton pickup
is seen on this spread—and remained
unchanged until 1953. The new-car sticker
price of this machine, which lived most of
its life in Virginia and has only 28,000
miles on the odometer, was $1,293. Dodge
built close to 60,000 B-3-B pickups and
panel trucks in 1951. The engine was an
inline six, with a displacement of 217 ci
and an output of 97 hp at 3600 rpm.

On this spread, a 1953 GMC. The slightly modified pickup classic—its two-tone paint scheme, its exterior mirror and its wheels are non-stock—lives in California's fertile Salinas Valley, where its owner uses it on a daily basis to transport produce from the fields to the area markets. The basic body style of the GMC pickup was shared with Chevrolet, and the design featured here was first seen in 1947. A restyling, which included a new grille and a one-piece windshield, was introduced in 1954. An all-new design, reflecting Chevrolet's trendsetting Cameo style, arrived in 1955. That year also marked the arrival of new power for GMC—a 287 ci, 155 hp V-8, borrowed from corporate neighbor Pontiac. But for 1953, GMC still relied on the faithful 228 ci flathead six it had used since 1939. Initially producing 80 hp, it now generated an even 100 hp at 3400 rpm.

International's prewar pickup, reissued in 1946, was replaced in 1950 by the company's first postwar design. Front-end styling now adhered to the fashionable pattern of the day, with pontoon fenders and faired-in headlights. The grille was a rather confused affair, with a collection of vertical louvers resting on a group of heavy horizontal bars. The grille was restyled for 1953. The louvers and bars were replaced by an oblong opening, which was traversed by a single chrome-enhanced bar. A bold nostril had been cut into the front end of the hood. The example seen on this spread dates from 1954. The grille was subsequently redone several times, until the basic body style was replaced by a totally new design in 1957. A respectable total of 85,000 units—all types counted—were built in 1954. The R-100 pickup cost $1,324. Fitted with the 220 ci Silver Diamond overhead-valve six, which featured rifle-drilled connecting rods and heat-treated aluminum piston rings, output was 100 hp at 3600 rpm.

8

Collecting the best of chrome-era beauties

By the mid-fifties, America's automotive manufacturers were engaged in all-out warfare. It was a battle for the affection of the customer, and the weapons were indeed bullets and bombs and rockets—even spears. Fortunately, they were all of the make-believe chrome variety.

As the styling war intensified, it inevitably spread to the pickup. The undisputed leader in the field was Chevrolet, which shocked the consumer—as well as the competition—with its introduction of the Second Series Advance-Design light-duty trucks on March 25, 1955.

Leading the field was a pickup called the Cameo Carrier. The limited-production half-tonner heralded Chevrolet's dazzling new look that pioneered the smoothside style. Also featured were egg-crate grilles, hooded headlights, fade-away front fenders, and a completely new cab sporting wraparound windshield and full-width rear window. The equipage was dressed in a special two-tone red and white scheme, which stretched to the interior as well.

Not only did this machine—and the entire family of splendid pickup creations it spawned as the 1956, 1957, 1958 and 1959 models arrived on the scene—appeal to the consumer of the fifties, it ultimately appealed to the collector of the eighties as well. Bud Bixler is a good example. The next twelve pages focus on the magnificent threesome of his collection.

By 1957, the styling of the Cameo Carrier had reached a pinnacle. As seen in this spread, the new look of the front end is dominated by the all-chrome trapezoidal grille, which added a new, distinctive growl to the appearance. Also changed was the hood badge, which had been enlarged. The bumper guards were optional, as were the dual hood ornaments and the sun visor. The new horizontal contrast band can be seen running all the way from the cab back to the tailgate. The full-view window was standard on the Cameo Carrier, but the rear bumper was an option. The colors are Cardinal Red with Bombay Ivory accent. Up front, coupled to the four-speed Hydra-matic, rests Chevrolet's potent Super Turbo-Fire top-of-the-line option, new for the year. This 283 ci V-8 powerhouse has a compression ratio of 9.5:1, features five main bearings and hydraulic valve lifters, and produces 220 hp at 4800 rpm.

With the Cameo, the Chevrolet stylists pulled all the plugs in their effort to create a dazzling vehicle. All the more remarkable was this emphasis on styling, since the object of their imaginative powers was basically a utility vehicle. But the trend of the beautification of the pickup had begun. Abundant chrome and curvaceous shapes had arrived. The photograph to the left affords a closer look at the front quarter of the 1957 Cameo, with its wide whitewall tires. The chrome hubcaps came standard on the Cameo, as well as on the Custom Cab. On the regular trucks, the hubcaps were painted Bombay Ivory, as were the bumpers. The enchanting trim ring, as pictured, was an appealing option. It was obvious that this machine was not meant for rough off-road work, but rather for on-road enjoyment. Chevrolet was generous with the application of its decorative bow tie, as seen in the photograph above, featuring the famous Cameo nameplate.

Creature comfort in the Cameo was every bit as luxurious as in Chevrolet's passenger cars of the same era. Design themes used in the company's main product line, such as the V-shaped speedometer, were carried through to the light-duty trucks in general. A special seat-cover material—red nylon fabric with white dots—was used in the Cameo. Adding to the cheerful roominess of the cab was the wraparound style of both the windshield and the rear window. Dodge had adopted the wraparound windshield in 1955, the same year as Chevrolet, but Ford was one year late in introducing the feature, while International did not jump on the bandwagon until 1958. Chevrolet's popular body style continued—with detail changes only—through 1959, and was shared by corporate cousin GMC in its Suburban. A total of 5,220 Cameos were built in 1955, 1,452 in 1956, 2,244 in 1957 and 1,405 in 1958. All models included, the five-year period saw more than one and a half million Chevy light-duty trucks hit the road.

*B*ud Bixler's 1958 Cameo is all original, unrestored, and was purchased from the first owner who drove it an average of just 3,000 miles per year. The color combinations are Polar Green with Glade Green accents. It sports the optional 283 ci V-8 coupled to the three-speed manual transmission. It also features the optional bumper guards, the rear bumpers and the sun visor. New for 1958 was the choice of two types of pickups. One was called the Stepside, which featured the traditional, exposed rear fenders. The other was referred to as the Fleetside, which had a slabsided box with built-in fenders. The latter type was actually pioneered by the Cameo, which used bolt-on plastic panels and a fiberglass bedliner to create this effect. In 1958, the Cameo had a base sticker price of $2,231. Today, a top-notch example such as Bixler's, featured in the photograph on this spread, is worth at least ten times that amount.

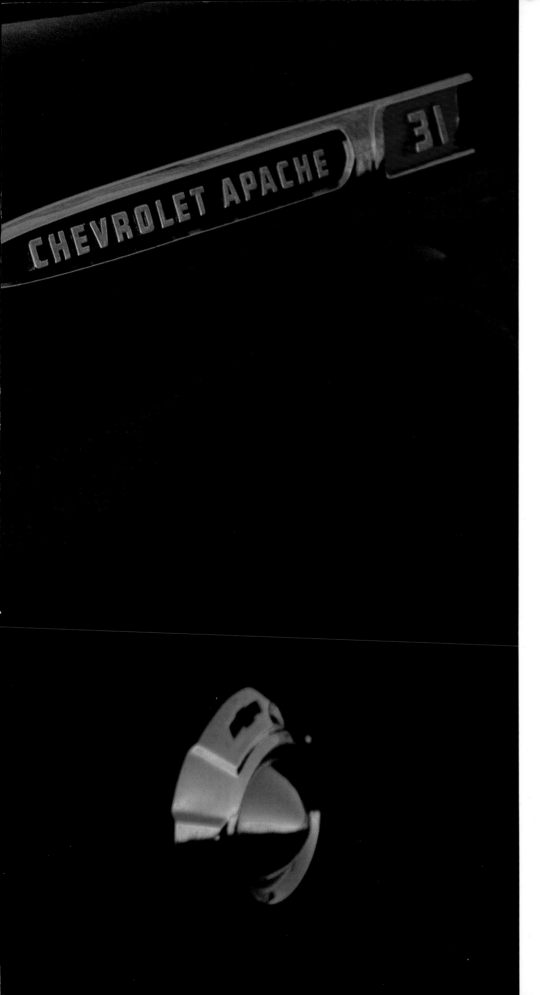

A new styling touch for 1958 was the use of dual headlights—part of a general redesign of the front end. The grille had been widened, and featured large rectangular parking and directional lights on each side. A thick bar embossed with the Chevrolet name connected these. Two thinner bars were stacked on top of the thick one. The entire steel extravaganza was held together by a chrome surround. The grille stayed unchanged for 1959, but a more elaborate chrome design surrounded the badge, located on the nose of the hood. The picture on the previous spread captures Bixler's 1959 Fleetside—also purchased from the original owner. The slabside look was now accomplished with steel panels, and not—as on the Cameo—with plastic panels. On this spread, a close-up of the chrome details on the 1959 Apache Fleetside.

79

*B*ud Bixler originally came from Iowa, where he was a farmer growing corn and wheat and raising cattle. In 1952, he sold out and moved to California. He worked as a plumber, a carpenter and a contractor before ending up selling Oldsmobiles in the late fifties. Now he lives in a small town south of Los Angeles, far beyond the reach of the big city—a place that gives him room to play with his trucks. Pictured here is his four-wheel-drive pickup, which was a factory-built unit first introduced in 1957. The Yukon Yellow is an original color. The wheels, on the other hand, are not standard—Bixler wanted wider tires for better traction. For the front drive axle, Chevrolet used a type manufactured by NAPCO. Transmission is a four-speed manual unit, with a low-low "granny" first gear and a floor-mounted stick. This, together with the stick of the two-speed transfer box, gives the cab interior the proper look, worthy of a heavy-duty machine of the traditional type. The rare survivor came out of Idaho, where Bixler went to pick it up.

81

9

Workhorses and other bewildering animals

The pickup comes in a multitude of shades and shapes. The concern is not just about the shade of Tartan Turquoise, however, but also about the extent of rust. And as far as shapes are concerned, it does not suffice to regard the more or less exquisite shape of a fender, but also that of a dent.

For the purpose of establishing the condition of a vehicle, collectors generally use the following code. Condition 5: restorable, needs complete restoration, not driveable, not wrecked, not stripped. Condition 4: good, driveable, needs only minor work to be functional. Condition 3: very good, fully operational original car or amateur restoration, presentable inside and out. Condition 2: fine, well restored, combination of well restored and excellent original or extremely well maintained original. Condition 1: restored to perfection or all original as new.

Now, there is also my own classification, colored by nostalgia and a certain attraction for the offbeat. In this system, a dented hunk of charm—like the one pictured on this spread—can score as high as a perfect restoration. A beat-up workhorse can cause more emotional bewilderment than a shiny show car with not a speck of personality.

With this foundation of anti-establishment sentiment, you should be properly prepared for the next eight pages.

*T*he charming 1947 Ford pictured in the photograph on the previous spread displays all the trademarks of a true workhorse. The many wounds, sustained throughout the long years of hard labor, have healed, although reluctantly, and the scars are still visible, superficially covered by several coats of loving care. Still dressed in its original blue livery, the 1953 GMC pictured in the photographs on this spread lives in the small, forgotten town of Halcyon, located on the central California coast. The picturesque machine stands as a perfect example of that well-proven theory of American back-country wisdom: "If it ain't broke, don't fix it!" All it needs is oil and gas, assures its contented owner, who uses the survivor to transport gravel, needed for the upkeep of the town's network of dirt roads.

Seen on the previous spread is yet another workhorse, a 1954 Chevrolet. Equipped with a camper shell of approximately the same vintage, this old-timer has seen several trips to Alaska. It now lives on the beach in Oceano, California, where its owner, Clement Eiland, parks it beside his small house trailer. Eiland is an old-timer, too, well past his eighties. Among a number of curious objects permanently housed in the cab, left, is a collection of cans containing rust remover. Pictured above, a 1950 Ford. Owner C. A. Paris, who lives on a walnut orchard in northern California, bought the survivor in 1951. He complains about his young nephews, who are learning to drive, and have little regard for the trees, or the truck, wounding the bark and denting the fenders.

*F*or a long time, Dodge stood out as a leader in the field of four-wheel-drive vehicles. Having begun experimenting with this technology already in the thirties, World War II and its urgent need for off-road machinery catapulted Dodge into fame. This vast experience was put to good use when peace arrived. On the facing page, a half-ton, four-wheel-drive Power Wagon from 1957. This was the first year for the new Forward Look styling. Owner Joe

Yaqui finds it the perfect machine for his profession—he restores old masonry buildings in California's Napa Valley. The truck was previously owned by an undertaker, who used it to transport dirt. Pictured above, another Dodge workhorse. This 1965 example, with its oversized headlight surrounds, is an excellent illustration of the creative imagination of Dodge stylists.

An old workhorse does not necessarily have to be in a beat-up, near-wreck condition. Ample illustration of this fact is found in the exquisite pickup featured on this spread, a 1966 Chevrolet C-10. Some folks are equipped with the enviable character trait of keeping their possessions in absolute prime condition. Owner Ken McGill of Rutherford, California, is such a man. He bought the Chevy new and, as is the habit of most such people, has even kept every one of the original documents. In spite of the show-quality condition of the truck, McGill has used it all these years in the maintenance of his vineyard, and at one time the pickup was operated as a tank truck in the field. The half-ton pickup is fitted with the long bed and the long, 127 inch wheelbase. Nearly 180,000 units were produced in 1966. The sticker price was just over $2,000. Today, according to a pickup price guide, the cherry old-timer would be worth close to four times as much—it pays to be particular.

Students of Ford pickups may pause in bewilderment at the sight of the 1976 F-350 pictured on this spread. The reason for the curious appearance of this vehicle is found in the fact that a half-ton body—its bed shortened by two feet—has been mated to a one-ton, 140 inch wheelbase chassis. This was done in order to create a breed able to handle the special towing problems posed by the sand dunes in Oso Flaca, California. The objects found stranded on this surfside vacation spot run the gamut from small family sedans to big motor homes. The need for traction on the part of the towing vehicle is met by huge sand-drag-type tires mounted on wide custom wheels. Power comes from Ford's eminently able 255 bhp, 360 ci V-8, coupled to a four-speed manual transmission. The owner-operator, proudly displaying the rebel flag, responds only to the nickname Outlaw.

97

10

The customizer—engineer, bold visionary, maverick

Should the workhorse pickup be allocated a category, however unofficial, the examples of this kind of vehicle are generally found to be in a sorry state—although charming—and thus would occupy a place near the bottom of the scale.

The subject of the following eight pages, the custom pickup, on the other hand, must be placed on or near the top.

What about the perfectly restored stock pickup? The amount of knowledge (historic facts, model peculiarities) as well as the degree of workmanship required to properly execute the restoration is considerable, and the product of such an effort admirable.

But consider for a moment the combination of skills required of a topflight custom builder. Not only must he or she, when it comes to craftsmanship, be able to perform on the same level as the stock restorer, but also must have superior knowledge of how the vehicle works, for the result of the customizer's effort often surpasses current technology.

Finally, add to this a needed healthy dose of artistic imagination, as well as the ability to visualize the unknown and untried.

The customizer indeed possesses something of the same obsession that drives the mountain climber. The obstacle—and the dream—must be conquered, for the sake of the conquest.

*F*ord's entry in the fifties' styling contest was the F-100. If Chevrolet's Cameos and Apaches indeed have a worthy competitor for the affection of today's pickup enthusiasts, this is the one! Introduced in 1953, and continually receiving facelifts, the F-100 reached an apex in 1955, with that year's clean and distinctive grille. For 1956, the grille was only slightly revised. This is the year of choice for customizer Elmer Eagles of Fairfield, California. The white machine, pictured on this and the previous spreads, is his most current

"child." It has won Best of Show on numerous occasions and is considered one of the most outstanding in California. Eagles is especially proud of the rear suspension, a Jaguar XJ-6 unit—all chromed. Up front he relies on a Pontiac unit, which provides power steering. The Jaguar-Pontiac combination ensures all-around disc brakes. The yellow machine is his previous child, now a driver. Under construction in his garage, still under wraps, is his new baby. It's a matter of continually extending one's limits.

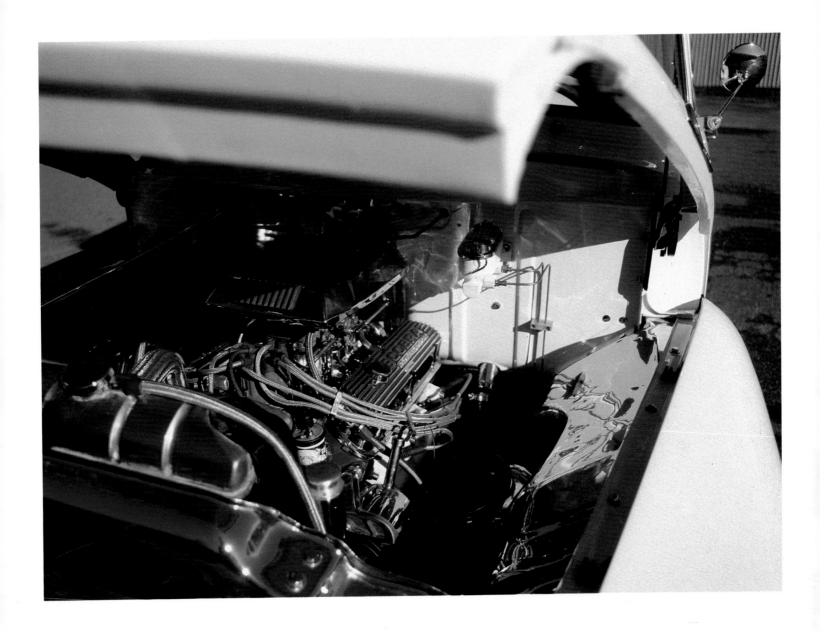

An F-100 pickup cost just over $3,000 in 1956. Today, a pristine example will bring almost three times that amount. More, if it comes with the optional panoramic rear window—just 6,200 units had that feature in 1956. It's no telling, however, how much a show-winner such as Elmer Eagles' F-100, its sumptuous interior pictured to the left, would bring. Regardless, it would be impossible to recuperate the hundreds of hours spent on such a project. It's truly a work of love. "Funny how things have changed," Eagles says. "In the old days you didn't drive a pickup unless you were a farmer or in some sort of business where you needed one. But now it's become an object of worship." The interior is velour-upholstered. The tilt steering column comes from a 1972 Pontiac Grand Prix. In the ceiling, also covered with velour, is mounted a Panasonic cockpit stereo. Seen above, the engine—stock inside, but highly customized on the outside.

*O*nly mildly customized, the pickups on this and the following spread represent a sector of the customizing scene where the object is to produce a dependable driver, not necessarily a show car. Seen here, a 1938 series 77 Willys. The manufacturer of this famous shark-nose design could trace its roots to the Overland Company, which began building delivery wagons in 1909. Hidden under the distinctive hood was a 134 ci four, generating 48 hp at 3200 rpm. The original engine is still the source of power in the featured truck, which was found in Kentucky, where it had received a street-rod restoration about twenty years ago. The wheels have been replaced for improved road worthiness, and sealed-beam headlights have taken the place of the original units. Pictured on the following spread, a 1946 Hudson Coupe Express pickup. For improved performance and reliability, the owner of this California beauty has replaced the original six-cylinder engine with modern Chevy power coupled to an automatic transmission. He has also replaced the rear axle; a 1970 Mustang unit was found to fit the original bolt pattern.

105

*W*hen Seth Doulton bought his 1956 Chevy about fifteen years ago, he had no idea the move would lead to a dramatic change in his life. While involved in the rebuilding of his new toy, he found the search for parts a most frustrating chore. Thus, faced with the problem, and finding others who were caught in the same predicament, he hit upon the idea of starting a business that would cater directly to owners of old pickups—fifties Chevys in particular. Setting up shop in Santa Barbara, California, and operating under the name Golden State Pickup Parts, Doulton has expanded the idea into a thriving business with a worldwide clientele. Although many exciting machines have passed through his hands over the years, Doulton has never let go of the original one. Under the hood of this beauty crouches a potent 427 Corvette engine, tweaked to its peak of performance. The simple design of the pickup classic is enhanced by the relatively restrained execution of the customizing. Twenty-three trophies testify to its excellence.

A couple of years ago, Derrill Pilkington decided the time was ripe to put all the ideas he had accumulated for his personal pickup into constructive action. He wanted a machine he could use every day, something nice and sharp, but nothing outrageous. He located a 1979 C-10 Stepside Chevy, and proceeded to give it a new paint job. The truck had already been lowered four inches by its previous owner, but Pilkington wanted more of the hunkered-down look, so he fitted eight-inch Cragar rims, wrapping them in beefy Goodyear Eagles. Red carpet was installed on the walls and floor of the cargo box, and a padded nylon tonneau cover was fitted for protection. Black and gold-leaf pinstriping established a color theme, which was carried through to the cab, with its plush carpeting and upholstery. Mechanically, he left the machine stock, but polished and chromed wherever possible. As a final touch, Pilkington had his own initials, and those of his sweetheart of thirty years, sandblasted into the corners of the side windows.

11

Low-rider versus high-roller

The sentiments that have moved the pickup from a thing of utility to a thing of play manifest themselves in many ways, all reflecting the preferences of each individual—as is to be expected in a society where the individual is king.

Consider, for example, the difference in intent of two particular groups of pickups and their owners, here referred to as low-riders and high-rollers. But first, the use of these descriptions requires elaboration.

The term low-rider has been associated with the machine so popular a few years ago, the star among the cruisers, a machine sending sparks flying every time its suspension hit the pavement. Here, however, the term describes the new trend among owners of mini trucks, that of lowering the vehicle to create a rakish silhouette.

The term high-roller does not exist, not in this context, but is used here for the first time—who knows, it may catch on—and describes the machines of owners who raise their pickups to enable them to clear obstacles.

Although both groups are fascinated by the engineering challenge, the ultimate goals differ. The low-rider spends a lot of time polishing and squinting and parading. The high-roller lives for the chance to get off the road and into the mud. It's all just as legitimate and worthwhile, and it's fascinating as a study in contrast.

*T*he photograph above, left, captures Allen Etchison and his 1978 Ford F-150 in their favorite element—muddy water. Etchison tailored the machine to his special needs by giving it a seven-inch lift, using four-inch blocks to raise the suspension, and three-inch hard-rubber bushings to give a boost to the body. He fitted a dual shock system, using four Rancho RS 5000 units up front and two in the back. HECO dual steering stabilizers completed the setup. The wheels are Enkies, and the tires 36.5/14.5x15 Four-Wheel RVTs. Under the hood, which once in a while needs to be raised to give the beast a moisture-repelling injection of WD-40—a scene captured above right—rests a 351/400 Midland. Etchison expanded the performance of this already potent power package by adding an RV cam and an Edelbrock Performance manifold, as well as Hedman Hedders. Breathing is facilitated through a Holley 600 cfm. On the following spread, the machine roars through the mud in a spine-tingling four-wheel slide.

*K*evin Martin drives his 1981 Toyota 4x4 as much as 150 miles just to be able to enjoy the element of his choice—sand, sand and more sand. The dunes at Pismo Beach constitute the largest mass of sand on the Pacific Coast. Once you are in its grips, surrounded on all sides by mountains of sand, you may think you have been transported to the Sahara. This is the country Martin was dreaming about when he outfitted his machine for the job. A three-inch body boost, and another three inches in the suspension, gave the clearance he wanted. The stock springs were exchanged for re-arched units from a three-quarter-ton Chevy. Four Rough Country shocks—he had fourteen at one time, but the ride got too unbearably uncomfortable—and one Rough Country stabilizer took care of the ride. A mushroom-shaped roll bar, topped off by a pair of Cibies, and a tailgate net, shown above, completed the picture. Captured in the photograph on the following spread, Martin and his mount take off on a flight to the limit.

*F*eatured on this and the following spread is one of the most outstanding mini custom trucks on the West Coast. The dazzling machine, a combination of engineering excellence and superb craftsmanship, is a 1975 Chevy Luv, owned and executed by Erik Adams of Atascadero, California. He bought the truck seven years ago, when he was just sixteen. It was pure stock at the time, had a faded yellow paint surface and ran on just two cylinders. Its poor condition, Adams thinks, was what got him going on a rebuild—or maybe it was something dormant in his personality. He started with the body, molding in the door handles, punching out the louvers and adding the fender flares. Finished with the base, he topped it off with a full-fledged, show-quality lacquer paint job, choosing a shade of metallic copper used by Porsche. Next came the engine. A V-6 Buick was his choice, coupled to a four-speed Muncie. The last step was the upholstery. All completed, it was finally time for the show circuit. Two dozen trophies attest to the success of the Adams creation.

123

*C*onfronted on the show circuit with the new craze of the tiltbed, Erik Adams went back home to lay plans for adding such an item. Two years later, he had it completed. But back on the show circuit for more trophies, he felt funny about having the tiltbed for no good reason, so he began racking his brain for a solution. One day he hit upon the idea of installing an independent suspension. Raise the bed and there it is, the chromed and polished unit from a Datsun 240Z. That made sense. It took another two years to plan the conversion, but just six weeks to execute it. Thus completed, his proud accomplishment was rewarded by a Best of Show at the Valley Run in Los Angeles' San Fernando Valley, where he competed with no less than 2,000 custom trucks—a feat that says it all about Adams' ideas and methods of execution. "Blue book for a '75 Luv is twelve hundred bucks," Adams jokes. "But I've receipts here for eighteen thousand! Figure that!" he adds with a grin. "Well, it's not a matter of money anyway, is it?"

124

*O*n this spread, Jon Simon's 1987 Nissan Hardbody takes mini fashion one step further. It features the ultimate tiltbed, referred to as a diamond, and able to swivel in any direction. Hydraulically actuated, and controlled via a hand-held console, a system of pumps and rams accomplishes the movements. The lowering of the vehicle itself was accomplished in the traditional way, through the application of blocks and the removal of springs. The wheels are Enkies six-hole units, fitted with Fulda Y-2000 50 series tires, pretty much the lowest profile available on the market. The color is stock, and called Blue Mist. The shell was custom-built by Supershell. A twelve-inch Formuling steering wheel improves the visual atmosphere of the cab, and a Pioneer compact disc with Rockford Fosgate amplifiers and speakers takes care of the audible ambiance.

ABZ- 7100

21.5